W9-BHJ-524

ME TOO!®
B O O K S

TWO BY TWO

THE STORY OF NOAH'S FAITH

By Marilyn Lashbrook

Illustrated by Stephanie McFetridge Britt

RAINBOW
STUDIES
INTERNATIONAL

El Reno, Oklahoma

Creating Colorful Treasures™

Noah's Ark has long been a favorite of young children. In TWO BY TWO, in addition to learning about Noah's faith and God's faithfulness, your child will have fun learning animal sounds and rainbow colors.

After each italicized question in the story, stop and allow your child to tell you what each animal says. Point to the animal words — such as *puppies, kittens* and *ducks* — and use them as beginning reading words. As your child grows, let him or her read more and more of the story to you. The "rainbow" pages at the end can be used two ways to teach colors. You may point and ask your child to say the color, or you may wish to say the color and ask your child to point to it.

Discuss in simple words how Noah believed God. Share with your little one your own faith in God.

Library of Congress Catalog Card Number: 87-60263
ISBN 0-933657-66-8

Copyright © 1987 and 1998 by Rainbow Studies, Inc.
All rights reserved. Printed in Mexico.

Art direction and design by
Chris Schechner Graphic Design.

1 2 3 4 5 6 7 8 9 — 02 01 00 99 98
Rainbow Studies International, El Reno, OK 73036, U.S.A.

Two By Two

THE STORY OF NOAH'S FAITH

Taken from Genesis 6 to 8

Noah was God's friend.
He believed what God said ...
God always tells the truth.

One day, God told Noah
there would be a flood.
"You must build
a great big boat," God said.

Nobody knew what a flood was.

But Noah believed God.

So he gathered enough wood
to build a great big boat.
Tap, tap, tap. Rap, rap, rap.

Noah worked very hard.
He made the boat
just the way God told Him to,
for Noah believed everything God said.

People came to see what Noah was doing.
When they saw the big boat,
they laughed and laughed.
"There is no water here!" they said.
"Where will you float your boat?"

Noah told the people what God said,
but they did not believe.
Noah went back to work.
He knew what God said was true.

One day the boat was finished.
"Now," God said,
"I will bring two of every kind of animal

to ride on the boat with you."
Noah waited for the animals to come.

The frisky puppies came two by two.
What do the puppies say to you? (bow, wow)

The soft furry kittens came two by two.
What do the kittens say to you? (meow)

The waddling ducks came two by two.
What do the ducks say to you? (quack, quack)

The spotted cows came two by two.
What do the cows say to you? (moo)

The curly-tailed pigs came two by two.
What do the pigs say to you? (oink, oink)

The wooly sheep came two by two.
What do the sheep say to you? (baa, baa)

The tiny mice came two by two.
What do the mice say to you? (squeek, squeek)

The great big bears came two by two.
What do the bears say to you? (grrrrrr)

The animals came two by two,
elephants, lions and monkeys, too.
Noah led them all into the boat.

"Bang!" God shut the door.
They were all safe inside.

Drip, drip, drip
the raindrops fell softly.
Splish, splash, splish.
They made puddles on the ground.

The lightning flashed!
The thunder cracked!
Down, down, down
the heavy rain fell.

Noah's boat rocked
a little this way
and a little that way.
It was starting to float.

For forty days and forty nights
it rained, and rained, and rained.
The water rose higher and higher.
And the big boat stayed right on top
with Noah and the animals safe inside.

Then something happened. Noah listened.
He did not hear the rain.

Slowly, very slowly,
the flood waters dried away.

One day, the big boat landed
on the top of a large mountain.

When God said it was time,
Noah let the animals out of the boat.
Two by two they marched
down the mountain
to look for new homes.

I will never again
cover the earth with water," God promised.
"And as a reminder,
I will put a rainbow in the sky."

Can you tell me the colors of the rainbow?
(red, orange, yellow, green, blue, purple)

Noah looked at the beautiful rainbow.
He knew what God promised was true.

And Noah was very glad
he believed God.

ME TOO!® B O O K S

Ages 2-7

SOMEONE TO LOVE THE STORY OF CREATION	**NO TREE FOR CHRISTMAS** THE STORY OF JESUS' BIRTH
TWO BY TWO THE STORY OF NOAH'S FAITH	**NOW I SEE** THE STORY OF THE MAN BORN BLIND
I DON'T WANT TO THE STORY OF JONAH	**DON'T ROCK THE BOAT!** THE STORY OF THE MIRACULOUS CATCH
I MAY BE LITTLE THE STORY OF DAVID'S GROWTH	**OUT ON A LIMB** THE STORY OF ZACCHAEUS
I'LL PRAY ANYWAY THE STORY OF DANIEL	**SOWING AND GROWING** THE PARABLE OF THE SOWER AND THE SOIL
WHO NEEDS A BOAT? THE STORY OF MOSES	**DON'T STOP. . . FILL EVERY POT** THE STORY OF THE WIDOW'S OIL
GET LOST, LITTLE BROTHER THE STORY OF JOSEPH	**GOOD, BETTER, BEST** THE STORY OF MARY AND MARTHA
THE WALL THAT DID NOT FALL THE STORY OF RAHAB'S FAITH	**GOD'S HAPPY HELPERS** THE STORY OF TABITHA AND FRIENDS

Ages 5-10

IT'S NOT MY FAULT MAN'S BIG MISTAKE	**NOTHING TO FEAR** JESUS WALKS ON WATER	**NOBODY KNEW BUT GOD** MIRIAM AND BABY MOSES
GOD, PLEASE SEND FIRE! ELIJAH AND THE PROPHETS OF BAAL	**THE BEST DAY EVER** THE STORY OF JESUS	**MORE THAN BEAUTIFUL** THE STORY OF ESTHER
TOO BAD, AHAB NABOTH'S VINEYARD	**THE GREAT SHAKE-UP** MIRACLES IN PHILIPPI	**FAITH TO FIGHT** THE STORY OF CALEB
THE WEAK STRONGMAN SAMSON	**TWO LADS AND A DAD** THE PRODIGAL SON	**BIG ENEMY, BIGGER GOD** THE STORY OF GIDEON

WE SEE!™ V I D E O S

VIDEOS FOR TODAY'S CHRISTIAN FAMILY.

51 animated Bible stories from the Old Testament ("In the Beginning" Series) and New Testament ("A Kingdom without Frontiers" Series) will provide your children with a solid cornerstone of spiritual support.

Available at your local bookstore or from:

Rainbow Studies International

P.O. Box 759 • El Reno, Oklahoma 73036 • 1-800-242-5348

RSI
Creating Colorful Treasures